D0090949

Common

Mistakes

Writers

Make

Eva Marie Everson

Lighthouse Publishing
of the Carolinas

COMMON MISTAKES WRITERS MAKE BY EVA MARIE
EVERSON
Published by Lighthouse Publishing of the Carolinas
2333 Barton Oaks Dr., Raleigh, NC, 27614

ISBN 978-1-941103-09-8
Copyright © 2014 by Eva Marie Everson
Cover design by Ted Ruybal, www.wisdomhousebooks.com
Interior design by Thomas White

Available in print from your local bookstore, online, or from the
publisher at: www.lighthousepublishingofthecarolinas.com

For more information on this book and the author visit:
EvaMarieEversonAuthor.com

Brought to you by the creative team at
LighthousePublishingoftheCarolinas.com:
Denise Loock

Library of Congress Cataloging-in-Publication Data
Everson, Eva Marie.
Common Mistakes Writers Make/Eva Marie Everson 1st ed.

Printed in the United States of America

Introduction

My writing journey began long before my publishing journey.

The first journey began with a book. Not writing one. Reading one. I can distinctly remember those first books that took me from my reality to another. They stirred my creative juices and often left me wishing I could stay within the realms of *that* reality instead of my own. Not that mine was so awful. To the contrary.

As a voracious reader, I developed a natural study of the craft. Understanding where to place quotation marks, commas, and indentations came with the storyline.

In 1997, when my publishing journey began, I had already acquired a natural knowledge of editing. I had much more to learn, of course. Things like not using *much* when it wasn't necessary. (See previous sentence.)

March 1997 marked the first Word Weavers (now Word Weavers International, Inc) critique meeting in Longwood, Florida. Five wannabe writers gathered around a dining room table and expressed their overwhelming desire to write professionally. I was one of them. All these years later, I am the president of this now-nonprofit organization of writers, and I have a respectable number of books with my name on the cover.

Many times I have been asked, "Will you look at my manuscript and give me your opinion?" Or, "Will you look at my manuscript and edit it?" I did that for a while, at no cost. Until the day I realized I spent more time editing other people's work for free than I did writing my own, which was my bread and butter.

And with that, the editing arm of my company grew fingers.

I find editing issues in nearly every manuscript, especially those of new writers. I made the same mistakes early on. After discussing the situation with a few of my conference director friends, I decided the time had come to offer "Common Mistakes Writers Make" as a conference workshop. And so I did.

After one of those conferences, an editor wisely asked, "Have you thought about putting this workshop into the form of a book or booklet?"

I had not—until that moment. (Insert smile here.)

What you are about to read is not rocket science. These pages are not filled with English Grammar 101 lessons (although one of the best things you can do for yourself as a writer is to find an old seventh grade English grammar textbook, read it, and complete the exercises). I don't claim to be an expert. Like most writers, I have to stop a moment and decide whether to use *who* or *whom*.

Farther or further.

That or which.

I have to get hit in the head by a dangling participle to recognize one. I often hear myself reciting, "Adjectives describe nouns and adverbs describe verbs."

(That's correct, isn't it?)

As I said, I don't claim to be the final authority on all the issues, but I know what I know. This book (or booklet) is but a small collection of editing "mistakes" I often find in the work that comes across my desk (and sometimes by my own hand). It shouldn't take long for you to read it, but when you reach the end of it, I hope you'll have had some aha moments. I'm writing conversationally, by the way, because I pretend I am speaking directly to you as I write, my friend. I'm basically telling you what I think I know.

If you'd like, you can let me know what *you* think (that is, if you are nice about it) by going to my website (EvaMarieEversonAuthor.com) and selecting the "contact" tab.

Eva Marie Everson

Part 1

The Basic Mistakes We Make
(And I do mean "we")

WEAK INTRODUCTIONS

The first thing an editor—whether acquisitions or content—or reader sees when they open your book to Page 1 is the beginning of what you are trying to say. Fiction or nonfiction—doesn't matter. If what you have written is weak, you've made your first common error.

Weak means that the writing is sloppy, the grammar is horrendous, and the hook is ... not there. Your hook—those first few lines and paragraphs—is critical. I often tell new writers that the first line of your book may not be the first line you write. If you are spinning and sweating over what those words will be, give it up and move on. Just start writing. Most of the time, my first line comes somewhere after I have finished typing the ninety-ninth page. Or I'm in the shower. Or asleep.

The flip side to weak writing is information dump. The writer erroneously thinks, "I have a lot to say and only a short period of time to say it, so let me say it all right here in the first few pages."

Wrong. Or, at the very least, misguided.

At first, life comes at us slowly, doesn't it? We leave the warmth of our mother's womb and enter a place of frenzy, yes, but then everything calms down. We nuzzle up to our mother's breast, she smiles down, we gaze up (who *is* this person?), and we feel only love and warmth. Over the course of the next few days and weeks, life is all about eating, sleeping, and being cooed at. No e-mails to answer, no calls to make, no chore list a half mile long. Life is easy.

At least for a time.

Think about it—if, at one day of age, we encountered everything we were meant to experience in eighty years … well, how much fun would that be? It wouldn't. And we'd run kicking and screaming right back into that safe womb if at all possible.

Later on, as our days become more numbered (and the hairs on our head are too), life comes quickly. At times, too quickly.

This scenario should be more like the middle of your book. The writing has to carry the reader from that hook to the satisfying conclusion and keep their attention in the process.

At the end of our lives, we should be able to see a common thread woven throughout. Whether you are writing fiction or nonfiction, this will be the way of your work. A common thread weaves and pulls the reader toward the message you are trying to communicate.

Don't try to do it in the first few paragraphs, pages, or chapter. If you do, your readers may run kicking and screaming back to the bookstore.

GRAMMATICAL ERRORS

Most of what this booklet contains, of course, falls into this category. Although I cannot cover all of these errors, I will do my best to cover the ones I find most frequently.

Remember when I said that finding a seventh grade English grammar book would be helpful? A couple of years ago, I went online in search of such a thing and found a book titled *English Grammar Demystified* by Phyllis Dutwin (McGraw-Hill, 2009). I not only found myself learning (and enjoying the learning at the same time), I also purchased one for my (then) sixth-grade daughter.

I don't know Ms. Dutwin and I'm not getting any compensation for talking about her book. And you certainly don't have to purchase it. But find something like it and refresh your grammatical brain a little. For many of us, seventh grade was a long, long time ago.

When it comes to spelling, there is little excuse. We have programs that will catch our mistakes—although if we mis*print* a word, we're on our own. For example, you intended to write *for* but you typed *or* instead. Spelling programs cannot catch that kind of error. In these cases, you must go back over your work, read it carefully, and look for spelling errors. Or, if you have a friend you trust to read your work and look for the mistakes, then—by all means—employ them for the task. When I read aloud, I catch more mistakes than when I read silently.

Too Much Irrelevant Detail

This goes back to what I talked about earlier with the information dump issue. Whether fiction or nonfiction, rabbit trails will lose your audience faster than subject matter they just don't care about.

We live in an information age, and that information comes at us faster than not. If your work runs down those illusive bunny trails, your reader's mind will soon be somewhere else. With all the competition out there, we—as writers—must worker harder than ever to keep our audience focused.

Speaking of audiences …

Not Understanding Your Audience

Who is your reader? Who are you hoping to reach?

And don't say "everyone." No book will reach

everyone. The bestselling book of all time is the Holy Bible, and even it is not for *every*one. (In its case, it *could be,* but not everyone thinks it's relevant.)

Know your reader. Know their needs. What kind of book do they like to read? If you are writing for readers who enjoy Amish fiction and fancy yourself an Amish fiction writer, but don't include any Amish fiction elements in your story ... well ... you've missed the mark.

If you are writing about prayer to those who are new to their walk of faith and your writing is something out of a doctoral program from the finest seminary in the land, you've missed your mark.

If you are writing to the parents of bipolar children, but you focus more on having the disease than on loving someone with it, you've missed your mark.

Understanding your audience requires that you focus continuously on what you want to say. Grab a sticky note from the pad, write your theme, your message, and your target audience on it, then post it near your work station. Look at it daily before you start to work.

Be Careful of the Big Words

If your audience is well educated, impress them all you want with the big words. But if you are writing to the average reader or consumer, don't.

That said, if you write fiction and your character is highly educated, you'll certainly want to sprinkle in the big words throughout. Smart folks who never speak above two-syllable words don't ring true. But if your character is a child, they must use the vocabulary of a child (again, unless your character is part of a Mensa group or something). If they, like Jethro Bodene of *The Beverly Hillbillies*, only graduated from the sixth grade, they must speak as such and their inner dialogue should convey that as well.

No Sense of Place

Whether you write fiction or nonfiction, the reader needs a sense of where you want to take them. In fiction, this is about setting. Setting is achieved not only through description but also through word choice.

Word choices also give nonfiction books a sense of place.

One of my favorite authors (okay, my favorite nonfiction author) is Robert Benson. His word choices bring me a sense of calm humor, peace, a deeper understanding of God's heart and mind, and a sense of quiet. Robert can talk about teenagers running through and in his home, yet there remains a sense of quiet peace because of his word choices.

Often when I teach a class on writing fiction and I want my students to understand fully the sense of place, I read the first pages of novels such as *Rebecca,* by Daphne du Maurier; *Love's Proof,* by Catherine Palmer (pages 3 and the top of 4); *The Red Tent,* by Anita Diamant; and *Cape Fear Rising,* by Philip Gerard.

You can go online and read the first pages of all of these (and a few of Mr. Benson's books) to see what I mean.

But remember, just because *you* can "see" the setting doesn't mean your reader can.

NOT KNOWING THE RULES FROM THE STYLES

There is, says Mignon Fogarty (known as "The Grammar Girl" and author of *Grammar Girl's Quick and Dirty Tips for Better Writing,* Holt Paperbacks, 2008), a difference between *style* and *rules.* For example, a period at the end of a sentence is a *rule.* But when it comes to things like spelling out numbers, serial commas (the comma before the *and* in a grouping of three things), the spelling out of

Bible book titles (such as *GEN* or *Gen* vs. *Genesis*), the use of ellipses vs. em-dashes—this has to do with *style*.

To distinguish the rules from the styles, you should own style handbooks such as *The Associated Press Stylebook* (often called "AP Manual of Style"), which is widely used by newspaper, magazine, and e-zine journalists, and *The Chicago Manual of Style* (often referred to as C-MOS or simply *Chicago*), which is used primarily by book writers (and is often considered a more complete stylebook).

These are not the only stylebooks out there. *The Christian Writer's Manual of Style* will answer those how-to-write-Bible-book-titles questions. *Publication Manual of the American Psychological Association* is the style manual for writers, editors, students, and educators in the social and behavioral sciences. The *MLA Handbook for Writers of Research Papers* is exactly what it says it is—a go-to book for students writing research papers.

Then, of course, there is *Elements of Style* by William Strunk Jr., a should-be-on-your-shelves book. In it we read the classic line taught at writing conferences everywhere: "to break the rules, you must first know the rules."

POV Shifts

This is, of course, primarily for fiction writers. We call it "head-hopping," and it is typically a no-no. (I say typically because a few works of recent fiction use this technique and have gone on to do quite well. However, the writing is *strong enough* that the back-and-forth between the thoughts of the characters doesn't slow the reading.)

If you read classic works of fiction, you'll see head-hopping everywhere. Not too long ago, I decided to read Erskine Caldwell's *Tobacco Road*. The POV shifts in the first few pages alone gave me a headache (though I enjoyed the work).

When you write fiction, get inside the skin (head) of one character and remain there throughout the scene. (This is obviously for third-person POV as first-person POV is only written inside the skin of one character.) To choose the character, ask yourself, "Who, in this scene, has the most at stake?" Crawl into that character's skin, see through their eyes, hear through their ears.

On that note …

Forgetting to Write Out of the Senses

Too often as I'm editing a piece, I realize that—whether the work is fiction or nonfiction—only the fundamentals are there. Even written from the correct POV, I feel little emotion toward the character (or subject matter) because I don't hear, see, smell, taste, or (physically) feel anything the character (or author) is hearing, seeing, smelling, tasting, or touching.

If you are in the moment as a writer, then you are *in the moment.* Put me, the reader, there too. Don't ask me to remain on the outside looking in. Readers, including me, read to escape to another world. Another time. Another … *character.*

Don't be afraid to be involved fully in your manuscript. At a Word Weavers group a few years back, a Jewish writer penned a scene describing a horror within the Holocaust. As is our method, the person to his right (which happened to be me) read the scene, and the person to the left began the critique. Everyone sitting in that circle cried openly as they, each one a Christian, told the Jewish writer how horrible they felt for him and his people. They gently critiqued the piece for grammatical errors and word choices. But when my turn came, I was less complimentary.

"Mark," I said, "I know you are afraid of wounding our sensibilities, but I couldn't smell the blood."

Everyone looked shocked. Everyone, that is, but Mark. He knew exactly what I was saying to him. "You're right, Eva," he said. "I was afraid to really crawl into the skin of my character."

"Don't be," I said. "I want to know what he could smell, taste, hear, see … all of it. I want to know if he grabbed the wool of his suit and if it felt rough to the touch. An odd thing to think about at such a time, but when we are in such a scene as this in real life, it's the odd things that we remember later."

He went back and rewrote the scene and, at the following month's meeting, we reread it. When we were done, I entered the nearest restroom and attempted not to vomit.

He had done the job right.

On the other hand … be careful when you write out of the senses that you don't *tell* vs. *show* what the character experiences via the five senses.

Instead of writing *he saw* or *she heard*, be creative. Let's say your character saw a car racing toward her. This one line gives the creative writer a lot of opportunity:

The car—rusty and rattling and expelling fumes—sped toward her. Her spine tingled, racing to her scalp like drumming fingers.

In one sentence, the reader sees, hears, smells, and feels what the character does.

Omniscient POV

This is commonly called "looking down from God's perspective" writing. While the writing can be lovely, it's considered faulty by many publishers. However, in more literary works, it's not unusual. Bottom line is that you have to know your publisher, your audience, and what it is you hope to gain by using this POV.

Flip-flopping Verb Tense

I don't remember the first book I read that deviated from the typical past tense point-of-view, but I do remember how difficult the reading was. After the first few chapters, I was "good to go." I also happened to be working on a novel, and I found the writing quite difficult. My tenses started shifting. I finally had to put my writing aside until I finished reading the book.

If you decide to go with present tense point-of-view, stick with it. Present tense vs. past tense is, simply put, the difference in:

I **walk** to the kitchen counter for my cup of coffee, all the while thinking I'd rather have a glass of Merlot.

and

I **walked** to the kitchen counter for my cup of coffee, all the while thinking I'd rather have a glass of Merlot.

SIGHING/LAUGHING DIALOGUE

"I just can't seem to do it anymore," she sighed.

Really? All that? In a sigh? Actually, your character didn't "sigh" all these words. Perhaps the character sighed and then *said* the line. Or said the line and then sighed. So, what you want to write is: *She sighed. "I just can't seem to do it anymore."*

Or, how about the character who "laughs" an entire line of dialogue? "And when I find him, I'll do to him what he did to me," he laughed.

Hmmm …

Written correctly: *"And when I find him, I'll do to him what he did to me." John's eyes bore into mine. And then he laughed. A horrible laugh. A laugh I'll take to my grave.*

BEGINNING TO …

This may only be a pet peeve of mine. When writers state that a character (or themselves) began to do something that they, in fact, continued to do, I wonder why it is necessary to say that the action began at all. *Just do it, already.*

Here's an example: *At the highway, we turned right and I* began to *accelerate.*

When I read this, I wondered, "Did you then take your foot off the gas and apply the brakes?" Reading on (this is from a piece I have edited), I realized that, no, the brakes were not applied. The character accelerated and kept going.

I changed the sentence to: *At the highway, we turned right and I accelerated.*

If your character (or in a nonfiction piece you or the person you are writing about) begins to do something and then stops, that's a different story.

I began to walk down the northern hall of the estate, but stopped when I heard a noise overhead.

NON-SPECIFICS

When you use action words, make them zing! By doing so, you give punch to your sentences—even those you feel are insignificant. Look at the difference in these two sentences and think about what you see when reading them:

Molly went to her mother.

Molly skipped to her mother.

See the difference? When I teach at writers' conferences, I often give the following exercise:

Write this sentence at the top of a page: SOME PEOPLE WALKED INTO THE ROOM.

What do you see here? Absolutely nothing.

Now try this: *Three women walked into the restaurant.*

Next, I send them off on their own for about ten minutes, asking them to think more clearly about these three women and the restaurant. Are the women tall? Short? Two tall and one short? Are they thin, fat, or in-between? How are they dressed? Approximate age? Does their jewelry jingle? Do they smell of perfume? Or are they vagabonds? And what about the restaurant? Is it a café? A French pastry shop? An elegant Italian restaurant with white linen tablecloths and dripping candles?

See the difference?

WAS (BY ITSELF)

I stop every time I see the word *was* before any word

ending in -*ing*. See if you don't think the second sentence of the following two examples is stronger.

*She **was walking** down the hallway.*

*She **walked** down the hallway.*

*He **was standing** in the middle of town, lost.*

*He **stood** in the middle of town, lost.*

It Was

First things first … avoid the "wazzies" as best you can. This is a weak word. *It* is another weak word because readers are often left to ask, "What is *it*?"

Put these two together, especially at the beginning of a sentence, and the whole thing starts off weak, probably never to gain strength as it goes along.

Yes, I know "It was a dark and stormy night" is a classic opening line, but—let's be honest—the line is weak. *What* was dark and stormy? The night.

Of course that doesn't sound nearly as lyrical, seeing as we have paid such homage to the line. Sadly, however, most of us cannot say who wrote it or from what work. (FYI: Edward Bulwer-Lytton is the author and the work is *Paul Clifford*, 1830.)

I'm certainly not going to try to undo the line

(known as *purple prose*) of this great writer, but let's look at a few more lines:

It was a dark and stormy night; the rain fell in torrents—except at occasional intervals, when it was checked by a violent gust of wind which swept up the streets (for it is in London that our scene lies), rattling along the housetops, and fiercely agitating the scanty flame of the lamps that struggled against the darkness.

What happens here is a classic case of "show, don't tell," which is another common mistake. If Bulwer-Lytton had simply begun with "Rain fell in torrents that night—except at occasional intervals ..." he would have avoided the "it was" and the telling vs. showing.

All right, all right. We wouldn't have this famous line, and I admit "Rain fell in torrents" is not memorable. But, hopefully, you get my point.

WRITE TIGHT

Don't use ten words to say what you could have said in two. In other words ... *write tight*. I know of a best-selling author who says that she pays herself a quarter every time she removes a word. Think of editing out unnecessary words as a "pay day."

Repeated Words

Repeated words are words or phrases that you, as a writer, tend to repeat every few lines. To find them, you must read your work out loud or allow a good reader or freelance editor who doesn't know what's coming to look at your work.

Here's an example: *She took the shampoo to the shower and placed it in the little wiry thing hanging from the showerhead. She loved this shampoo. It was the shampoo her mother had used and when she washed her hair with the shampoo, she smelled her mother. Or, more precisely, her mother's hair.*

See the problems? I can easily overlook the two *showers* in the first sentence (*shower* and *showerhead*), but *shampoo* is used to the writer's detriment. (And we won't even talk about the *it was* here.)

Written tighter: *She took her favorite shampoo to the shower and placed it in the little wiry thing hanging from the showerhead. When she'd stripped down and stepped behind the thick plastic curtain, she turned on the water, removed the bottle's cap, and inhaled. For a sweet moment, she imagined holding her mother … breathing in the scent of her hair. Which was, of course, why she had never changed brands. Silly to some, maybe, but this was all she had.*

THAT AND HAD

That and *had* can often be eliminated from sentences, thus causing your work to be tighter.

That: I suggest reading the sentence out loud with, and then without, the *that*. If the sentence makes sense without it, cut the word.

With the *that:* She said *that* they were going to the mall tomorrow.

Without the *that:* She said they were going to the mall tomorrow.

What do you think? Is the word *that* necessary? It's not, no. So delete it. (Allow me to let you in on a secret. When I first wrote the sentences above, I wrote: *She said that they were going to go to the mall tomorrow.* But when I edited the line, I removed both *that* and *to go*, which made for tighter writing.)

Had often lets us know of something that happened previously. Let's say I'm telling you about an incident that took place last week, and I write: *I had thought to go the movies, but decided instead to take a nap.* If I establish the time frame, I don't need to use the word *had.* Example: *Last week I thought to go the movies, but decided instead to take a nap.*

Another mistake I often see is a writer who is giving backstory. *Had* tends to show up in nearly every sentence. Once the writer has established the timeframe, they can leave the *hads* out.

WEAK WORDS

Weak words in writing are words like *very, much, so, just, only*, and the *to be* verbs, such as *am, is, are, was, were, be, being, been*. Think, too, about the nondescript words like *big, small, tall, short, thin, fat*. Be careful, too, of unnecessary words. An example would be: *The shouting faded away.* The word *away* is not necessary. If it fades, it goes away … (I have a short list of my favorite unnecessary words at the end of this book.)

Writing with the fewest number of weak words means you have to work hard at your craft. This may not be what you want to hear. Perhaps you are saying right now: "I have the talent. What do I need with all these rules?"

Well, let's face it—if everyone could write—and do it well—we'd all be Stephen King.

CATCH PHRASES

I received an e-mail from my content editor once with a single question. *Eva*, she wrote, *do you realize how many times you wrote "a bit" in this manuscript?*

I did a global search of my project, typed in "a bit" and discovered that those two words were, indeed, my "catchphrase." I wrote things like:

She turned a bit.

He walked a bit down the road.

A bit, a bit, a bit.

I had no idea. Soon enough I noticed the catchphrases of other writers, typically while editing or in critique. The best way to find *your* catchphrase(s) is to read your work carefully. Or, join a critique group such as Word Weavers International (www.Word-Weavers.com) and ask your critique team to do an honest search.

The "Ly" Words

"Ly" words are adverbs used as modifiers, whether in prose or as dialogue tags.

Mary ran quickly to the corner store.

Better: Mary sprinted to the corner store.

"Leo, do not trek mud on my clean floors," his mother said tersely. Leo knew she meant it.

Better: "Leo, do not trek mud on my clean floors." His mother spoke through gritted teeth and Leo knew she meant it.

In the second example, the writer almost doesn't need the "spoke through gritted teeth." If the mother's personality has been established, the reader knows exactly how those words were spoken. (As a mother, I cannot image saying those words with glee, can you?)

Doing Two Things at Once

This is so common in writers, especially new writers. We watch movies and television shows and often, as writers, we see the scenes playing out. Because of that, we sometimes write two things happening at one time.

Still, our characters cannot do two things at once. Allow me to give you an example:

Walking across the room, she opened the door.

I'm not a physics expert, but I know those two things happening at the same time are not possible.

What is the correct way to write it?

She walked across the room and opened the door.

Let's look at another one:

Laughing hysterically, he told another joke.

If he laughed hysterically, how could he possibly tell another joke (that I could understand, at least)?

He laughed hysterically, then told another joke.

REFUSING USEFUL CRITIQUE

As the president of Word Weavers International, and as a member, I have spent close to twenty years giving useful critique and receiving it as well. As someone who has learned the value of critique, nothing burns me up more than hearing someone shun what I know to be honest, heartfelt words of help.

Critique is *not* criticism. Proper critique should never leave the writer feeling crucified. Done right, critique points out the areas where a writer is strong *and* where a writer is weak. When the critique is accepted with an open mind and heart, the writer can go back to the drawing board and strengthen that last area.

Think about it—does an athlete in training ignore the weak areas of their sport? My daughter was a National Champion roller skater. If she could not get her double axel, she practiced it over and over and over again. When her coach said, "Use your core muscles to pull up," she knew those core muscles had to be made strong and kept strong. The same is true for a writer. We must strengthen our weak areas.

To extend this "just a bit" (yeah, I know what I wrote),

what shocks me more is hearing an editor give awesome advice to a newbie writer at a writers' conference, then hearing that newbie writer become argumentative. I can mentally hear the editor saying, "And off you go …" every time.

Forgetting the Era (Fiction Writers)

Fiction writers often forget what era their characters live in, using words and phrases in dialogue that have not been formed yet. For example, someone in 1920 wouldn't say, "She's off the chain." Rather, they may say, "I fear she's lost her mind."

And, for example, remember that not everyone in the early 1900s owned a car. Or had a phone. Or indoor plumbing. And not everyone in the early 1950s owned a television set.

As you read over your first or second drafts, look for errors in era. Check to see when certain phrases were popular or even came into being. Another example: the term *having a blast* (meaning, having a good time) became popular in the 1950s. *Groovy* came into play in the 1960s. Right? Wrong! The first time something was called *groovy*—meaning hip and trendy—was in 1937.

So before you write these "signs of the times," be sure

to look them up and, in doing so, discover their origins.

Not Following Submission Guidelines

I've worked on anthologies with easy-to-follow guidelines and watched writers—some of them seasoned—fail to color inside the lines.

"Send an article of no more than 1000 words" does not mean send 1500, even if you think those extra 500 words are the best ever penned since the creation of ink and parchment.

"Deadline, May 1" does not mean that on May 1 the writer can send an e-mail asking, "Is this for real or can I have ten more days?"

"All submissions must be sent through an agent" does not mean you can squeak by without one.

I have found that, to editors, writers who submit within guidelines are valued as gold.

Excessive Exclamation Points

When I first entered the publishing world, a wise acquisitions editor said to me, "If you have a work of 100,000 words, we should see no more than two exclamation points. You have five on the first page alone."

I have never forgotten that. What he meant was

that my *words* and the actions of my characters should denote whether or not they are yelling, screaming, or bellowing. Now I use exclamation points sparingly … so much so that *Shift-1* keys are hardly ever touched on my computer.

Part 2

Spelling and Grammatical Errors

ACCIDENTALLY OR ACCIDENTLY

If you type either of these words into a Word document, neither will come up as "wrong." However, one is.

Accidental means "by mistake."

An accident is what happens when two cars collide. Or, you drop your spoon into a bowl of soup—not meaning to, of course—and splatter beef vegetable all over your new white tee. (Want to guess what I did today?)

Because *accidentally* (which is how the accident happened) comes from *accidental*, then this is the proper/correct way to write the word.

However, because both have been used for a while, both are *accepted*. Still, only one is *correct*.

AFFECT OR EFFECT

I've read every rule on this imaginable, and I still get confused. Based on the questions and misprints of my clients, I'm not alone. So let me make this easy.

Affect (typically) is used as a verb and means "to produce an influence." Or, more simply, to "to effect."

Poor language skills will affect your writing.

The rain will negatively affect our party.

Effect is (typically) used as a noun and will oftentimes have a, and or the in front of it. It means, "a change that results when something is done or happens."

The effects of poor grammar are documented.

An effect of spending too much time in the sun is sunburn.

ALRIGHT OR ALL RIGHT

Here's an easy way to remember how to write this correctly: *Alright is never all right.*

ALL TOGETHER OR ALTOGETHER

All together means that everyone (all) is together.

Once our flight had landed in Dallas, we found our luggage all together *in the baggage claim area.*

The lions were all together *at one corner of the reserve.*

Altogether means "completely."

Have you gone altogether nuts?

The price of the skirt with the blouse minus the twenty-five percent was $49.99, altogether.

The lions that were all together at one corner of the reserve were altogether impressive.

ALTHOUGH OR THOUGH

Although both are correct, at the beginning of a sentence, a reader by nature will see *though* as *through*.

BLONDE OR BLOND

A *blonde* is a female with *blond* hair.

However, a male with *blond* hair is still a *blond*.

COMPLEMENT OR COMPLIMENT

Complement (with an *e*) means "to complete."

Compliment (with an *i*) is what you get when you are doing something well, or what you say to someone who does something well.

DOUGHNUTS OR DONUTS

This isn't a common error, per se, but it came up recently in a conversation, so I thought I'd add it.

Doughnuts are made of dough, fried slap silly (thus the *nuts*), and absolutely scrumptious when they're hot (and even when they're not) and glazed. Or sprinkled with cinnamon and powdered sugar—I'm not that picky.

Donut is an abbreviation of *doughnut* and, therefore, not proper unless you are on Facebook or Twitter and want to say, "Today I ate 2 donuts and promptly all my daily allotment for calories." That's fine.

Delicious, actually.

ENTITLED OR *TITLED*

To be entitled means that you are due something or owed it.

As the oldest daughter of our mother, I am entitled to her wedding rings.

A book, paper, document, or magazine article, is titled.

The title of the book is Common Mistakes Writers Make.

I cannot tell you how many times I have seen these two words used incorrectly. Or, to be more exact, spoken incorrectly, which is why I believe we often see them written wrong.

Wrong: *She bought a book entitled* The Road to Testament *by Eva Marie Everson.*

Right: She bought a book titled The Road to Testament *by Eva Marie Everson.*

FARTHER OR *FURTHER*

Both words deal with distance. *Farther* is typically

physical distance while *further* refers to nonphysical, or figurative distance.

How much farther from here do we have to drive?

If he takes this argument much further, I'm going to explode.

FEWER OR LESS

We say this incorrectly so often, we end up writing it incorrectly as well.

Fewer is used when counting in numbers.

I have fewer *red buttons than white ones in the jar.*

Fewer *and* fewer *people come to the monthly meetings as time goes by.*

Less is used when counting in nouns or mass.

I have less *of a chance of winning than you do.*

If I had less *of a mess in my knitting basket, I'd have room for new skeins of yarn.*

FOREWORD OR FORWARD

A foreword comes at the beginning of some books. Some call it the preface. Remember, the foreword consists of *words* that come be*fore* the rest of the book. Seems simple enough, but all too often I get e-mails from writers asking, "Should this book have a forward?"

Historic or *Historical*

If something is historic, it is important to human history. Historical refers to things from the past.

Lincoln's Gettysburg Address was a historic *event from the nineteenth century.*

The book about Lincoln's Gettysburg Address is considered by most readers to be historical *nonfiction.*

Samuel Clemens's childhood home in Hannibal, Missouri is of historic *importance to the writing community.*

Samuel Clemens's childhood home is filled with historical *mementos.*

Internet or (small i) internet

For years, this debate ended with a resounding, "Capitalize the *I*!" This is because, in most instances, *Internet* came from proper names concerning the World Wide Web. In time, however, the capital *I* was dropped because the word became less proper and more generic.

Along that same idea, the word *tissue* is often given the name *kleenex* even though *Kleenex* is a product name and should be capitalized. The word *gelatin* is often referred to simply as jello, although *Jell-O* is a product name and should be written as you see here.

IT'S OR ITS

Even Microsoft Word's autocorrect gets this one wrong from time to time. *It's* is a contraction for "it is." *Its* is possessive. I know, I know. Sometimes when we look at *it's* we think "possessive" because of the apostrophe. A little trick I played on myself years ago was to type, over and over, *it's* while saying "it is." It worked. I never typed it wrong again.

It's time to leave for the symphony. (It is time to leave for the symphony.)

The clock had a crack along the front of its face.

LIGHTENING OR LIGHTNING

Lightening is a bleaching agent or the reduction of weight, such as "To lighten your load, bring the bags in two trips instead of one."

Lightning (no *e* after the *t*) is that bolt of electricity from the sky that is usually followed by a rumbling of thunder.

LOOSE OR LOSE

Loose means the opposite of tight.

Lose means that you have misplaced or forever lost something.

Lying or Laying

I lie. Two little words I repeat in my head when I'm trying to remember the rule.

To lie means to rest. Recline. To lay means to put something down. Or someone.

I decided to lie down for a while.

I had to lay the baby in the crib.

As simple as that seems, we have misused these two words for so long, the misuse has become common. Add to that, the option of using the words in the simple present, simple past, present participle, or past participle verb tense and the whole matter becomes confusing. On these occasions, the little seventh grade grammar book comes in handy.

Of

The use of the word *of* is often unnecessary.

Eva Marie is the daughter of *Betty and Preston.*

Eva Marie is Betty and Preston's daughter.

This is the home of *Cynthia and Jim.*

This is Cynthia and Jim's home.

As I said, the word *of* is *often* unnecessary. This means sometimes you will want to keep it.

Just recently my daughter, who is an editor on my team, sent an example of the word *of* being used that was artistic. *Should she, as an editor, change it?* We both agreed she should not.

Okay or *OK*

Okay is a word. *OK* is an abbreviation. If you wish to impress *this* editor, write the word out, especially in dialogue.

Parental Names

"Fixing" this is a constant in my editing work.

When writing mom/mother/mama/momma or dad/father/daddy (and this goes for grandmother/grandfather), as proper names, the first letter is set in upper case. When referring to a parent or grandparent in general, the first letter is set in lower case.

Sarah, did you know Mom is planning to come for a long visit?

My mother is planning to come for a long visit.

After Daddy died, I found it difficult to drive past his old home.

After my father died, I found it difficult to drive past his old home.

Did you know that Grandmother bought a new car?

Our grandmother bought a new car.

PRINCIPAL OR PRINCIPLE

If something is principal, it is most important. (A little trick I use is to remind myself that *A* comes first in the alphabet, making it the "most important" letter of the twenty-six.)

The principal household expense for us is our mortgage.

Also, when speaking of the "head" (or most important person) of a school or learning institution, the word to use is principal.

Dr. Phillips is the principal at my son's elementary school.

There are other ways to use *principal* as well.

The principal *star in the film was Cary Grant.*

The principal *offender in the burglary case was the older of the two men.*

Principle also has several meanings:

A principle is a fundamental law, doctrine, code of conduct, or rule.

The principal *explained the school's* principles.

If it helps at all, principal can be either an adjective or a noun, but principle is always a noun.

Seasons of the Year

Again, this is an incredibly common error I find in the manuscripts I edit. The seasons of the year are *not* capitalized. (Repeat: they are *not* capitalized.)

Every year holds a spring, summer, autumn, *and* winter—*unless, of course, you live in Florida.*

The exception (you knew there would be one, right?) is when the season is part of a proper name, such as Spring Fling, Summer Olympics, Fall Festival 2013, or Winter Clearance Sale (my personal favorite).

Speaking of fall … is the correct word *autumn* or *fall*? They're both correct. One is more formal (actually, more British) than the other. Personally, I think which one you use is a matter of preference. *I prefer* autumn because 1) I think the word is prettier and 2) I like the song *Autumn Leaves.* But *your* preference should be entirely left to you.

Scripture or *scripture*

Because I edit a lot of faith-based work, I see this mistake a lot.

The definition of *scripture* is two-fold:

A sacred book of writings

Passages from a sacred book of writing

When we make reference to the Bible, we are referring to the Scriptures. If we are referencing specific passages from within the Bible, we refer to the scriptures (meaning the verses).

Within the Scriptures, *I found several* scriptures *about money.*

Sunday school or Sunday School

I see this more times than I care to edit. So, let me ask you a question. If Christians gathered to sip on coffee, nibble on doughnuts, and chat about their weekly Bible study on Monday, would you capitalize the *s* in school? Probably not. But there's something about the fact that this "school" is on Sunday that makes us want to cap the *s*. Don't. The correct way to write it is thusly: Sunday school.

And on that note, the correct way to write Bible study is without capping the *s* in *study*.

While we're talking about the things of God, if something is "like God," it is godly. Not Godly. The correct word to use when talking about things from the Bible is biblical. Not Biblical.

The chain of disasters seemed of biblical *proportions and altogether* ungodly.

THEN OR THAN

Then is a moment in time.

First I will go to the grocery store, and then *I will come home and cook hamburgers on the grill.*

Than is a word used in comparison.

I would rather eat raw fish than *have to go out with him tonight.*

THERE, THEIR, OR THEY'RE

When I first started editing, seeing the number of times writers get this wrong came as a surprise. (I almost wrote "a bit" of a surprise.)

There is a place. But be careful with there. Use it too often and you'll find yourself writing in generalizations.

Okay: *I love the fair. I used to go* there *every year.*

Better: *I love the fair. Every year brought higher anticipation for a spin on the Ferris wheel.*

Their is possessive.

Their *boat is a pontoon. Mine is a Tracker.*

They're is a contraction, a more casual way of saying "they are."

They are coming at noon for lunch.

They're coming at noon for lunch.

Who or That

This is a pet peeve of mine. People (and, in my mind, animals) are "who" and things are "that."

Incorrect: *The little boy that came to the door is my son.*

Correct: *The little boy who came to the door is my son.*

Correct: *The carton of eggs that sat on the shelf too long went bad.*

Your or You're

Believe it or not, this is a mistake I also see quite often.

Your is possessive.

Your *boat is a pontoon. Mine is a Tracker.*

You're is the contraction, a more casual way of saying "you are."

You are kidding me, right?

You're kidding me, right?

Who, Whom, That, or Which

The first part (*who* or *whom*) is as easy, typically, as knowing whether or not to use *he* or *him*.

He (or she) = who.

Who took Martha to the party?

He took Martha to the party.

Martha was taken to the party by whom?

Martha was taken to the party by him.

That or *which* is a little more complicated (well, for me, that is) and is based on the kind of clause you wish to use. Ask yourself this question: is the clause necessary (or important) to the sentence? If your answer is yes, then use *that*. If the answer is no, then use *which*. Most often *which* is preceded by a comma.

In these economic times, my car, which drinks gas like a man left to die in the desert drinks water, should be traded in.

Why did I use *which* instead of *that*? Because I can take out the clause and the sentence still has value.

In these economic times, my car should be traded in.

Let's look at *that*.

The shoes that go with this outfit are uncomfortable.

The meaning changes if I take out "that go with this outfit."

The shoes are uncomfortable.

See? I need to be specific about *those particular*

shoes. Otherwise, it could be any number of the pairs I have in my closet.

TOWARD/BACKWARD/FORWARD OR TOWARDS/BACKWARDS/FORWARDS

Placing the *s* at the end of these words is more common in the Queen's English. American English drops the *s*. On that note, you will often see a different spelling for words such as *catalogue* (Queen's English) and *catalog* (American English), and *dialogue* (Queen's English) and *dialog* (American English). Personally, I prefer the Queen's English when it comes to words such as these. You will have to make your own preference.

THINGS YOU MIGHT WANT TO LOOK UP

We have a few sayings in our English language that have *changed* over the years, but I'm not sure that makes them *correct*. When you hear a common phrase, look it up to see if it has been used correctly.

Two examples come quickly to mind:

The good Lord willing and the creek don't rise.

This saying, which means "hopefully," is—written correctly—the good Lord willing and the Creeks don't rise. Creeks referred to the Native American tribe known as Creeks.

She was chomping at the bit to leave the house.

Well, it makes sense, doesn't it? But the saying, which means "anxious," is—written correctly—*She was champing at the bit to leave the house.*

Other sayings, such as *I'm going over this with a fine-tooth(ed) comb,* can be written both ways. To my knowledge, the saying didn't begin one way and then become another. The difference simply comes in whether or not you think the comb is *fine-tooth* or *fine-toothed*, with neither answer being correct.

THE THINGS THAT MAKE ME SMILE

I cannot help myself. (Oh, there's another one. The word is *cannot*, not *can not*.)

When I see the following phrases in the work I am editing, I smile. Then I correct.

Nodded his head. There is only one thing on your body that nods, typically, and that's your head. Simply write: He nodded.

Stood up. There is only one way to stand and that is up. Simply write: She stood.

Stood to her feet. Only one thing to stand to, unless your character or the person you are writing about is an acrobat. Again, simply write: She stood.

Sat down. Only one way to sit and that's down.

Simply write: He sat.

Blinked her eyes. Only one thing to blink. Simply write: *She blinked.*

Balled up his fist or *clenched his fist.* A fist is a hand balled up or clenched. One cannot ball up or clench what is already balled up or clenched. Simply write: *He fisted his hand* or something along those lines.

Thought to myself. Unless you are a professional mind reader, the only person you can think to is yourself. Simply write: *I thought …*

I'm sure there are others like these. Most writers I know have their own list.

Now, before you panic, *don't.* Recently, I flew … somewhere … and, bored, reached into my carryon for a book to read. I pulled out one of my own, which I intended to give as a gift to my hostess. Seeing as it was too much of a struggle to put it back and get the book I had been reading, I opened *This Fine Life* and read.

Because a couple of years had passed since I had read the galley of the book (what we writers get before the manuscript goes to print), I found myself fairly fascinated by the story. In other words—I got into my own book.

When I reached one of the last chapters, I laughed out loud. Lo and behold, I had written (and apparently not edited): *She nodded her head.*

I say this to let you know that even the pros mess up now and again.

Mostly again.

55954164R00033

Made in the USA
Lexington, KY
07 October 2016